WHISPERS

A Collection of Poems

Adeola Oyekola

Whispers
All Rights Reserved.
Copyright 2026 by Adeola Oyekola

This book is a collection of original poems and reflections.
All poems, thoughts, and expressions are the creative work of the author.

No part of this book may be reproduced, transmitted, or stored in any form or by any means—electronic, mechanical, photocopying, recording, or otherwise—without the prior written permission of the publisher, except in the case of brief quotations used in reviews, scholarly work, or critical articles.

The reflections contained in this collection explore faith, growth, and the quiet spaces where human experience meets divine grace. The poems are works of literary expression and imagination. Any resemblance to specific persons, events, or situations is coincidental and interpreted through the lens of poetic storytelling.

First Printing, 2026

OLABOOKS INTERNATIONAL
MY BOOK · MY PASSION

https://www.crystalcdc.net/published-books

ISBN: 979-8-9897213-5-1 (eBook)
ISBN: 979-8-9897213-4-4 (Paperback)

PRINTED IN THE UNITED STATES OF AMERICA

Dedication

This piece is dedicated to all the low moments
that would not have the final word.

Contents

Prelude 1

   Live Above Them 3

Part 1 5

   Upon Arrival 7

   After the Question 9

   The Habit of Answering 12

   Respect 14

   If He Talked Too Much 16

   It Will Not Silence Him 18

   Not in a Moment 20

   The Box 22

   What He Sees 23

Part 2 25

   Within His Musings 27

   Am I a Fool? 28

   Mercy 30

   Out of Place 31

   In Disarray 33

   In Distress 34

   He Tried! 35

Part 3 37

   Hope Is Not Lost 39

   Far Away He Leads Me 41

It's a Win-Win 43

Look Beyond Them 45

Make Me Understand 46

It's Another Day of Waiting 47

Birthdays Are the Best 49

Mourning 51

Insecurities 52

Spirit Beings 53

Who's That Lad? 55

PRELUDE

Live Above Them

Live above all low moments
Structured to tear you down
Live above trials and temptations
Orchestrated to test and frustrate you
Raise your head high
And desire to elevate your state

Do not shut down
Do not whimper
Do not be suppressed
But be certain
In the estate you desire
Be strong in your will
Be determined to rise
Above the stagnant water
Designed to contaminate you

You determine who you are
Not the circumstances or the situation
He says, she says, they say
What do you say?
What is He saying?
These are your resolutions

You live for all moments

Weather in the valley

Or on the mountain

When that moment comes,

One way or the other

That moment will come,

You stand tall

Never afraid

Because you are wired

To defeat them all

PART 1

Upon Arrival

He slipped into the meeting space, a little late
though earlier than his usual lateness.
The room was already breathing
with answers and knowing faces.

Then suddenly his name …
the moderator called.
It fell into the room
like a rock dropped into water.
His mind scattered
down a river inside him
where words refused to swim.
Blank.
Yet, his mouth betrayed him,
silence spilling expressions such as a confident river
flowing in the wrong direction.
Long.
Certain.
Completely wrong.
And the room contained the moment like a mirror.
The question stood there waiting for him,
as though presence meant preparedness,
as though walking in was the same as being ready.

But he had just arrived.
What embarrassed him most
was not that he did not know,
but that he was made a spectacle
of his incomplete arrival.
Some call it participation.
He calls it being placed
where anyone could stumble.
He had barely entered.
That should have mattered.

AFTER THE QUESTION

Then the session ended
with the correct answer
exaggerating the wrong.
They had their fill.
The disapproval hung over the air,
the embarrassment looming in his hair.
Then his name, again…
but this time, softly.
He was sent on an errand
from the back to the front
so he could show off the feathers of dishonor
they had just given him.
"Here, take this to the front and bring it back."
What icing on an already beautifully decorated cake.

But he listened.
He delivered the message
like a well-brought-up child.
"Never disrespect an elder."
But he had just been their moment,
their example,
and their spectacle.
Eyes followed him.
So did murmurs,
body language,

unspoken judgment.
It was indeed
a day to remember for him, for them,
for he had always minded his own business.
But the scripture says there will be stumbling blocks.
He Spoke Anyway
Perhaps he should have been quiet.
Perhaps silence would have saved him
from the long road of a wrong answer.
He could have lowered his eyes,
and let the question pass
akin to wind over still water.
But the moment came quickly,
and he answered.
Yes, his words wandered, confident and mistaken.
For one moment,
the room contained his error
like a brittle thing.
But regret is not the whole story
because he spoke in a world
where many shrink from the sound of their own voices.
He opened his own without fear.
The answer may have been wrong,
but the bravery was not.
He may rethink the words
that left his mouth that day,
but he will never apologize
for the confidence
that sent them forward …

to speak freely,

and to stand without trembling before a room.

That, too, is a gift.

And even in error,

he will honor it.

He could have lowered his eyes,

let the question pass

akin to wind over still water.

Once, that is exactly what he would have done.

There was a time when his speech lived in hiding—

a time when fear sealed his lips together

and he buried his thoughts deep inside himself.

He would have ingested the moment whole

and punished himself in silence

for words he was never brave enough to say.

But that was another version of him.

The path that built his boldness

was not formed in a single moment.

THE HABIT OF ANSWERING

His life moves quickly.
Questions arrive all day long …
problems to untangle,
decisions to make,
people waiting
for clear words.
He is used to answering.
Even when the problem
has not fully formed,
he steps in and gives it shape.
So, when his name was called,
he did what he had always done.
He answered.
Not because he had studied the moment.
Not because he had raised his hand.
Not because he came prepared
to enter that conversation.
He had barely settled.
His thoughts were still arranging themselves
like books not yet placed on a shelf.
He was minding his thoughts
not theirs.
But that part of him that refuses to lose a moment,
that part that answers problems
before they fully arrive stood up first.

The words came out

strong,

certain,

and confident.

Then he finished speaking.

And only then did he collect the manual and look.

The page stared back at him with the silent truth

he had not yet seen.

That was the moment he realized what he had done to himself.

He had allowed the version of him

that solves everything

to speak where it was not needed.

He was not one of them, not at that moment,

not in that circle.

Still, he knows this much:

the instinct to respond is not his weakness.

It is the evidence of a life spent

thinking clearly,

speaking boldly,

and refusing to stand silent

when he is made a spectacle.

Next time, he may not answer the question,

but he will not condemn

the part of him that answered.

RESPECT

They are older.
They can pick on people.
And when an elder
asks you to speak,
silence is not always freedom.

Respect sometimes asks the voice
to rise even when the heart
would rather remain seated.
Did he answer because honor
has its own language?
His words may have wandered,
confidently yet mistaken.
It was respect standing up
before comfort had the chance.
Some may call it a mistake.
But he knows what it was:
a lifetime of learning
that when elders call your name,
you do not guard your silence.
You offer your voice.
But they saw him
the way elders sometimes do
not as he is,
but as someone younger,

someone to summon,

someone to answer,

someone to send,

and someone useful.

That's why they made him a spectacle,

twice within a moment.

The room moved on,

but the moment

stayed with him.

IF HE TALKED TOO MUCH

Later, someone said
perhaps he talked too much
as if one's voice had been searching
for the center of the room.
But if that were true,
you would have seen it.
Hands do not hide
when they hunger for attention.
If he were keen to speak,
his arm would have risen
before his name was ever called.
The room would have known his intention.
But his hands were still.
He had just arrived,
his thoughts quietly his own,
resting where no one
had asked them to go.
He was not reaching
for the question.
The question reached for him.
And he answered
not because his sound needed the air,
but because respect answered first.

Some say people talk too much.
But those who truly know
the gift of expression also know this:
a voice that speaks freely does not need
to chase the moment.
When it wishes to speak,
it raises its hand.
His did not.
His name was simply called.
And the voice he carries,
the one he worked hard for
refused to hide
once it was summoned.

IT WILL NOT SILENCE HIM

Perhaps the moment
was meant to stop him.
A small spectacle
placed in the middle of
a room, a token
to stay quiet next time.
But his life does not move that way.
His days are built on voices
conversations,
decisions,
clarity spoken across tables
and across phones.
This is what he does.
He speaks.
He solves.
He builds.
His work is not borrowed.
His work is an invention:
businesses born from ideas
that refuse to stay silent.
So, one wrong answer in one room
cannot close the doors
he has opened for himself.
If anything,
it sharpens his firmness

because the life he lives
was not built on silence.
It was built
on courage,
on speaking clearly,
and on stepping forward
even when the moment is imperfect.
Perhaps he would not have been
that brief spectacle if he had been
exactly where he was expected to be.
But life is larger than a single room.
And his voice, the one that feeds his work,
builds his ventures,
and carries his ideas forward
will not be shut down by a moment
that lasted only minutes.
If anything, it reminds him
to work harder,
build higher,
and keep moving,
because a life built by his own hands
cannot be undone
by one question
asked too soon.

NOT IN A MOMENT

Some may think
success lives
in the quick answer,
in the sudden brilliance
of a moment.
But that is not his story.
The things he has built
did not arrive
in a wave of a moment.
They were carried slowly
through long days,
late nights,
quiet thinking that
no one ever sees.
And above all,
by the grace of God.
Not by being called suddenly to speak.
Not by a question that appears
without warning.
The work that lasts
does not grow that way.
Ideas that hold their weight
are not accidents.
They are turned over
again, and again

in competent hands
until they are ready to stand.
So, if a moment
caught him unprepared,
it says little
about the life he has built,
because what he builds
is not born in haste.
It comes
through prayer,
through thought,
and through work
that continues long
after the room grows quiet.
And whatever success
has found his path
has never been
the reward
of a single moment.
It has always been
God's grace
walking patiently
beside his labor.

THE BOX

A moment can become a box.
Four quiet walls built quickly
from surprise,
from judgment,
from words
spoken too soon.
And suddenly,
the moment shuts around him a box.

But some boxes do not trap you.
Some push you inward
into the quiet place
where tones outside grow faint
and another voice waits to be heard.

So, he stepped into the prayer room.
Not the one with walls and doors,
but the one the soul enters
when it needs to breathe again.
Moments may try to corner us,
but prayer is always larger
than the room.
And what people
think they have closed,
God is always opening.

WHAT HE SEES

If this moment were carried to the eyes of Jesus Christ,
He wonders what He would notice first.
Not the question that threw Him off.
Not the answer that wandered.
Not the quick verdicts written quietly
in the corners of the room.
People see a moment
and build a story from it.
He spoke too quickly.
He spoke too long.
He did not know that
judgment travels fast
when a moment
is all that is visible.
But He, who formerly silenced
a circle of accusers
in the pages of
the Gospel of John,
does not measure people
the way rooms do.
He looks deeper.
A man just arriving,
his thoughts still gathering
like birds returning
after a long flight.

A name called
before his mind had time
to sit down.
Respect rises first
because honor
was taught long ago.
And so the words came,
self-assured yet misplaced.
But heaven does not weigh a soul
by a single answer.
The room may remember the mistake.
But God remembers the heart.
And one heart that answered
out of respect is not the spectacle
people think they saw.
It is simply a human moment
held tenderly in the mercy of God.

PART 2

Within His Musings

He ponders how he shall express
a core of thankfulness
when his inner self is
brimming with anxieties.
Within his consciousness,
rivers of promise flow,
yes, torrents of conviction,
certainly, currents of serenity.
But this calm is short.
As his spirit wanders
and the rough seas surface,
subsequently, he feels lost
in his mind.
Streams of shame flow,
no, floods of worries,
my goodness, torrents of scorn.
And his core is full of disgrace
and scorn, hmm.
It all culminates in unrest,
a choking sensation.
The turmoil and raging agitation,
the weight and trail
of hardship and loss.
How can he transition to his peace?
And in reality, he has control
to select peace
that originates from faith and hope.
His devoted mind rests in Him.

AM I A FOOL?

Am I a fool
to believe the dream?
I am thoroughly immersed in it.
I cannot withdraw.
I have faith in the Lord, yes, I do,
but how do I remain in it?
Am I a fool
to have faith without reason,
or to love blindly?
Why did I love blindly,
and trust without hesitation?
Eyes shut to reality,
eyes sealed to reason.
My eyes remain shut to man's thoughts,
blind to the risks.
Yes, it is the peril,
the peril that now breaks my heart.
Why have I chosen to walk on a thin line?
The audacity and bravery
that bite hard right now.
Where is the exit?
Is it that direction or the second one?
The rapid and simple route
or the constricted passage?
I will stick to his preference.

I will not lament through the constricted gate.

I will persist in believing,

because He never falters.

He will guide me there,

to His abode of quietness.

The inferno that rages in me will not engulf me.

The immense deep will not claim me.

All the days of my appointed time

I will wait on the Lord

until my transformation arrives.

MERCY

Mercy, where are you?
Are you real?
Mercy, where are you?
It is necessary for you
to act on my behalf.
You have to speak up!
I am here, anticipating and wailing,
crammed up in a nook,
my tears flowing freely.
Will you disregard me?
Did you not notice me?
How could you not spot me?
I want you right away, I say right away!
Mercy, oh mercy, you must locate me.
You cannot stay out of sight for long.
You are mercy, and you must come to my aid.
That's my sentiment.
But you must think differently,
if you are not here yet.
I plead for mercy.
Lord, I implore you, have mercy
on me, and in my weaknesses.
I long for you, Lord, I long for your mercy!

OUT OF PLACE

The dungeon is not his place.
How did he even end up there?
He's isolated in obscurity.
Will aid come?
He absolutely needs it.
Will aid come?
In an aisle so distant,
in the center of a conflict arena,
how do you justify a victory when you're not accused?
Regardless of his frame of mind,
he believes in God for help.
But what if it never comes?
Think, what if it never comes?
The platform you are anticipating,
the shift you foresee will happen.
Why would you even believe it will happen?
What if it never occurs?
Sir, what does the "dungeon" feel like?
You lingered there and remained?
Did you entertain the possibility that He would not respond?
What if there were no transformations?
Did you at any time feel out of place?
But Job received an answer,
which means
it is not fitting

to reflect out of grace.
It is out of place
to bask in disgrace,
and out of place
to suppose help will not come.

In Disarray

How will he shatter the curse?

He has attempted it many times.

He can't break the curse.

It's incredibly hard for him.

This mountain sits in his chest resembling stone,

be removed and thrown in to the sea!

Hmm, did it listen?

He certainly made an attempt.

His faith seems like it is not working,

perhaps not this time.

His being is in severe distress,

because his mountain refuses to move.

How much time will it take for him to remain in this state?

The mountain is set for an appointed time.

He might as well start to chisel it down.

It's not likely that his legs could be of good use,

but his mouth and heart can.

How about He stand firm in faith?

He speaks his faith with fire,

then the mountain will hear him,

and it will indeed be removed.

IN DISTRESS

What should he do?
Now that he is so down,
get up and pray,
but he is exhausted;
talk to a friend,
but they won't respond;
immerse yourself in work,
and remain fixed on your purpose.
Never linger in bed for too long,
engage your body, mind, and spirit,
walk with faith.
Yes, your fate is established by faith.

He Tried!

He tried!
He tried.
Yes, he did try.
The thought won't go away,
because it's a part of him.
Indeed, he tried
to push away the fears,
to erase the memories,
and to make things feel the same again.
He still tried.
How on earth will this go away?
He labored.
He vented.
He ran and ran.
Indeed, he tried, but it won't go away.
In his corner,
or what do you call it?
In his shed of gloom,
he tried
to ease the fears,
the pain,
the unknown world of loneliness.
When they shut him down,
and make him the victim,
when they are truly wrong.

There isn't any mercy anywhere,
but he remains on his feet.
He tried.
Lord, he tried
to do what You taught him,
to remain calm and believe,
believe that his troubled waters
will soon calm down.

PART 3

Hope Is Not Lost

Hope is not lost.
Hope is alive.
Living is a lie
when hope is denied.
The farther you look,
the deeper the desire.
Hope is at home.
Hope is hidden.
In it lies redemption.
Perhaps life changes.
In hope lies our future,
the future in which we find rest.
Hope is a friend.
Hope is comfort.
If life gives you a seat,
then your heart is at rest.
Why live in hope?
In it, there is peace.
Hope is a treasure.
Hope is a pleasure.
If you have to wait for it,
then wait for it.
It is for an appointed time.
Hope in your career.
Hope in your dreams.

Hope for the future.
For indeed, it is the nature
of confidence to be for an appointed time.
What does hope look like?
Light? Breath? A small flame? Morning?
Live in your hope.
Live in your dreams and visions.
And declare into your hope
that all is well.

FAR AWAY HE LEADS ME

Oh, far away I will go,

as thunder threatens the cloud,

and fire cracks within the furnace.

In the rage of the sea,

fear is born.

So far away, He leads me

into the darkest valley

and a shadowed tunnel.

Who can survive?

Though it thunders,

there is no rain.

The ocean rumbles,

but none is lost.

The fire cracks and sparkles,

but none is burned.

What, then, is my fear?

A loud noise that holds nothing.

Oh, I can make such noise too,

and it will mean something.

I can dare the thunder

still the raging sea

and quench the fire.

I have the spirit of a sound mind,

the sword of the Spirit.

I shall trample them all under my feet

and cut them down with my sword.
That's all you've got, threats?
I am the child of the King.
I hold power over you.
Under my feet, you remain trampled.

It's a Win-Win

When I follow,
it's a victory.
When I obey,
it's a breakthrough.
For who shall stand
against the Highest and win?
I will stand for the Highest and win.
He never sleeps nor slumbers.
I sleep and slumber.
If He were my friend,
I will not worry.
When I sleep, He hides me.
When I fall, He picks me up.
When I am down, He stands up for me,
defending me from the enemy.
You see, it's a win–win…
always on the winning side.
Do I have to worry about anything?
No, for when He opens my eyes,
I see an army all around me,
looking after my needs.
I am indeed a treasured child
who has everything at my beck and call.
Never again will I worry.
Never again will I fret.

Indeed, I am sorry for the days I worried:
sorry for myself, because it was wasted energy.
From now on, I worry not.
I bask in the wisdom of knowing
that I have more than enough angels supporting me.
I am the boss.

LOOK BEYOND THEM

Behind the veil,
beyond the shade,
right beneath it, you will see
the treasure.
Yes, past the waves,
beyond the tears,
beyond the fog,
underneath the rock lies
the riches.
What if there's nothing beyond?
What if behind the door is
nothing but emptiness?
What if, yes, what if?
Then, the wealth…
look beyond the fear.
Look beyond the doubt.
Look beyond the fault.
For right within you
lies the treasure you seek.

MAKE ME UNDERSTAND

Make me understand
why life is so cruel.
Make me understand
why life is a struggle.
Do you really understand
why life makes you cringe in fear,
and the unknown turns out to be okay?
Can you make me understand
why life holds you bound in hate
when you could be free in love?
Hmm, there's a season to grieve,
a season to ponder,
a season to endure,
and maybe a season to lack.
But in all seasons, there is love.
Don't you feel it?
Yes, there is love.
It's the *iroko* tree you need
to lean on at all times.

It's Another Day of Waiting

When will the wait be over?
Only God knows.
How long will I wait for an answer?
Only God knows.
Listening to His words,
singing hymns,
praying daily,
and meditating on His words
have been keeping me strong.
But for how long?
Only God knows.
Perseverance is not a joke.
"Wait on the Lord.
Don't you dare step out of
His commands.
If He says it,
He will do it."
Yes, sir!
You are right.
But for how long?
Only God knows.
Getting busy while waiting
is the best option.
Can you write?
Can you sew?

Can you knit?
Can you read?
Do that and
pray, fast, prophesy, decree, and declare,
and wait for it.
For only God knows
when your answer will come.

BIRTHDAYS ARE THE BEST

Birthdays are the best,

never meant to be the worst

for those who celebrate.

If you don't celebrate,

what does that day mean to you?

A number? Nothing more?

Have you achieved anything?

How long did it take?

When do you stop to celebrate yourself?

Indeed, there is a meaning

to your existence.

Some pregnancies never made it.

How old are you?

Someone younger

just passed away!

There is a purpose

when you survive the worst

and you could have also passed away.

But why birthdays?

It's a remembrance.

Never forget.

It's a remembrance of one or more years,

a remembrance of grace,

a remembrance of your purpose.

It's a remembrance of the day you were born:

your first victory,
you pushed through,
eternal registry,
everlasting memory,
a remarkable arrival, worth celebrating.

Mourning

She left me,
and I am left alone.
Can screams relieve the pain?
Does crying, wailing, and
weeping wash away the pain?
What about sleeplessness?
Watch all night and wait
for the dead to come back?
The vigil didn't work?
Maybe rolling back the hand
of time would do the magic.
Is it possible?
No.
It's a time of sorrow…
a time of weeping, longing, wailing.
What helps in a time like this?
Maybe nothing.
Everyone finds a safe place.
I find mine in Christ.
My faith produces my fate.
He said, "Live one day at a time."
Each day has its grace.
"May the Grace of the Lord Jesus Christ,
the love of God,
and the sweet fellowship of
the Holy Spirit
be with us now and forever. Amen."

INSECURITIES

Oh, my! A stain on my shoes.
I can't stand up.
All eyes are on me!
Why is she gazing at me like that?
Could it be my clothes are transparent?
Allow me see …
no, it's not that.
It's my purse. It doesn't match my shoes.
Or my wig, it's too short.
I should have worn the long one.
Oh, my, she's holding a Birkin!
I'd better hide my coach!
I should have known to stay home!
How about you find a purpose?" He asked.
Where are you?
Where are you headed?
I am obtaining strengthen and meaning,
and staying focused on my life.
My insecurities are my misfortunes.
But you can be confident.
You can love you.
You should love where you are.
That's true!
Step by step, I will get there.
I am clay in the Potter's hand.
Ouch! It's only a molding.
I will be the finest when I am ready.

SPIRIT BEINGS

A product of Easter.
It couldn't have been better.
Made in spirit, wrapped in spirit, moved by the Spirit.
From gory to glory,
from being slain to the Savior,
from miry clay to a miracle.
A seed is sown.
There's a rebirth.
Wake up from your slumber.
Your life is declared.
Declared in war,
promoted in fury.
Stand up for your rights,
for you must take it by force.
Promotion only comes
when you declare war,
to claim what was lost,
stolen, and buried.
Look up to the cross.
The Savior has done it all.
Suffered for you.
You need to claim your rights.
Nailed to the cross,
spat on,
beaten and buried.

Did He stay buried?
He rose up.
Why not get up?
Stir up your spirit.
Use your power
and decree your victory.
You breathe.
You can war.
You will win.
It's your time.
It's your race.
It's your success.

WHO'S THAT LAD?

Who dropped into the pit so dark?
I suppose I know him.
The one who carries on like
he has knowledge
that exceeds everybody else's.
At times, it seems like he commands the world
and strides with his ego lifted high.
He got what he deserves.
This is his final.
He will never rise again:
a blemish, a shame.
Hmm, couldn't believe
it finally happened.
But he endures.
He whimpers.
He toils.
Yes, because when you descend,
it's your phase in the deep valley.
When you ascend,
it's your moment to thrive.
But when you trip,
and you pay attention
to all the lies that try to tie you down,
you remain in the deep, low valley.
Gird your loins.

Gather your bits.
Love yourself
and persist through it.
Experience the weather,
for the greens
flourish in the misty valley.
It's a plus.
Triumph and defeat
are two faces of a coin.
When defeat presents itself,
just a flip will transport you from it.
Persist in trusting.
Keep faith
you have Jesus,
who is the companion
closer than a brother
because you need Him
all the time.
You need Him particularly in moments
when minding your business
did not work for you,
but someone dragged you
into the miry muck!

www.ingramcontent.com/pod-product-compliance
Lightning Source LLC
Chambersburg PA
CBHW051459140726

47987CB00006B/2792